The Christian Testimony of Major-General James Ewell Brown Stuart

Copyright © 2005 by Edward DeVries
ISBN: 9798555054777

Published by
Dixie Heritage Press
www.DixieHeritage.net

FOREWORD
by Colonel J.E.B. Stuart IV
U.S. Army, Retired

As the great-grandson of Major-General James Ewell Brown Stuart I have often been asked for an opinion of this great man's legacy to the nation, and how he should be remembered. Although my answer has changed, as I have grown older, one central theme has endured through the years: He was a man who fought for a cause that he deeply believed in with tenacity and a steadfast commitment that is remarkable by any standard.

My great-grandfather knew how to organize and lead men in combat, his assessment skills were second to none, and he had no equal in technical proficiency in the development and use of cavalry. As a result, he played a major role in developing the doctrines that still shape mobile warfare today. If you were to visit an Armored Cavalry [tank] Regiment today and ask the Commanding Officer to describe the unit's strategy he would describe it in terms very similar to those developed by General Stuart during the War for Southern Independence.

Many books have been written about my great-grandfather, his military career, his rise through the ranks to command of the Confederate Cavalry, his great exploits in battle, the victories he won, and even his tragic and untimely death in the service of his country. But to my knowledge, this is the first and only book to be written entirely on the Christian faith and personal character of General Stuart. While many authors have written on all that my grandfather did, Dr. Ed DeVries has written this book to help show us the inner faith and spirit of this great man.

General Stuart possessed an integrity, personal character, and convictions of conscience sadly lacking in many men today. He was a faithful Christian man with a strong biblical belief. While General Stuart did not fear men or bullets, he did fear God, and this was the true reason for all of his successes in life, both as a man and as a soldier. J.E.B. Stuart's faith was his "center of gravity." It was the foundation upon which all of his life and actions rested.

This short, well put together book, composed largely of excerpts from my grandfather's own writing, will give the reader great insight into the faith and character that was Major-General James Ewell Brown Stuart.

J.E.B.

December 22, 2005

TABLE OF CONTENTS

Foreword *(by Col. J.E.B. Stuart IV)*..................3

Part One - The Christian Testimony of J.E.B. Stuart as Evidenced by his:

Chapter One: Godly Heritage..............................7

Chapter Two: Student Record...........................9

Chapter Three: Faithfulness on Frontier Duty.........11

Chapter Four: Fearlessness as a Soldier................13

Chapter Five: Always Fighting for the Glory of God..15

Chapter Six: Faithfulness to the Local Church..........17

Chapter Seven: Efforts to Seek Conversions...........21

Chapter Eight: Faithfulness to the Bible and Prayer....25

Chapter Nine: The Way He Lived the Scripture.........27

Chapter Ten: A Man without Vice........................31

Chapter Eleven: His Personal Letters...................35

Chapter Twelve: Official Military Reports..............39

Chapter Thirteen: Personal Poetry......................41

Chapter Fourteen: *Deathbed Assurance of Faith* 43

Chapter Fifteen: *The Eulogies Given* 45

    Part Two -

Chapter Sixteen: *In My Hand No price I Bring* 49

Chapter Seventeen: *A Godly Legacy* 53

End Notes 55

CHAPTER ONE

GENERAL STUART'S CHRISTIAN TESTIMONY IS EVIDENCED IN HIS GODLY HERITAGE

James Ewell Brown Stuart, commonly known as "Jeb" or J.E.B. Stuart from the first three initials of his name, was born in Patrick County, Virginia on February 6, 1833. On each side of his family, he could point to a line of ancestors who had served their country well in war and peace and from whom he inherited his high ideals of duty, patriotism, and Christian faith.

In "the year 1726, J.E.B. Stuart's great-great-grandfather, Archibald Stuart, fled from Londonderry, Ireland, to the wilds of Pennsylvania, in order to escape religious persecution."[1] Upon arriving in the "new world" the Stuart's were instrumental in the establishment of the Tinkling Spring Church, where "the graves of the immigrant and his wife may still be seen."[2]

J.E.B.'s great-grandfather was Major Alexander Stuart, "commander of a Virginia regiment at the battle of Guilford Courthouse in the Revolution....He became a man of wealth and influence in Virginia."[3] Major Stuart was also one of the founders of Washington College.[4] Major Stuart invested not only his influence and wealth but also his faith into the organization and building of the college. As a result. Washington College was considered to be one of the nation's premier Christian Colleges in the early years of American history.

J.E.B.'s father was raised a Presbyterian and his mother was raised as an Episcopalian. As a result Biographer Burke Davis describes J.E.B.'s youth and home life as having been "religious."[5]

J.E.B.'s father was "a fine singer" who would often "sing in church."[6] J.E.B. and his brothers also liked to sing and they would often sing hymns together.[7]

J.E.B.'s mother was a very godly woman who would always insist that her son maintain a high level of Christian devotion and moral purity. She saw to it that he received a Christian education.[8]

> It seems that Jeb, in God's grace and providence picked up the best from both his father and his mother.[9]

As an adult, J.E.B. Stuart would later recall the words of David the Psalmist:

> *"yea, I have a goodly heritage."* -- Psalm 16:6

> *"thou hast given me the heritage of those that fear thy name."* -- Psalm 61:5

CHAPTER TWO

GENERAL STUART'S CHRISTIAN TESTIMONY IS EVIDENCED IN HIS STUDENT RECORD

At age fifteen, J.E.B. enrolled in Emory and Henry College, a Methodist school.

"Jeb was converted when he was sixteen, at Emory Henry College during a revival that swept that college in that year, and he became a member at that time of the Methodist church."[10]

The Reverend J. Steven Wilkins noted that:

> Although his conversion occurred when he was rather young, it was very solid.[11]

While attending college J.E.B. also liked to attend Gospel singing schools. These singing schools were conducted throughout the 19th and early part of the 20th century by traveling teachers who would teach the students how to sing hymns and read "shape" notes. J.E.B. wrote to his cousin Stuart about attending one of these schools:

> There is a singing school in town at this time taught by J. B. Wise. He has a great many scholars both male and female - among others I am a scholar.[12]

Upon graduating from Emory and Henry College J.E.B. received an appointment to the United States Military Academy at West Point. While at West Point Cadet Stuart was a favorite and regular house guest of Commandant Robert E. Lee.[13] Mrs. Lee noted that at all times, "He has the manners of a true Virginian."[14] Cadet Stuart was in fact so well-mannered that he insisted that Mrs. Lee chaperone all of his dates.[15] J.E.B. Stuart was both Commandant and Mrs. Lee's "favorite cadet"[16] because they both considered him to be "a zealous and earnest Christian."[17]

Stuart was well known by all of his fellow cadets at West Point. They nicknamed him "Bible Class Man."[18]

CHAPTER THREE

GENERAL STUART'S CHRISTIAN TESTIMONY IS EVIDENCED IN HIS FAITHFULLNESS AS A SOLDIER ON FRONTIER DUTY

Upon graduation from West Point, Stuart was assigned to frontier duty in the western territories. Historian John Dwyer notes that during his days on the frontier Stuart was known for, "His God and his practical jokes."[19]

In her popular biography Mary L. Williamson notes that while on frontier duty:

> ...the only books that he had to read during the long, weary days were his Prayer Book – which was not neglected – and his Army Regulations.[20]

John Dwyer noted that even as a young man, Stuart "knew every line"[21] of his prayer book.

The following account, which is from, of all sources, a biography of "Stonewall" Jackson, clearly illustrates that J.E.B. Stuart was different from the other soldiers on the frontier. That which made him different is also what earned him the respect of his peers:

> Stuart knew his removal as company Quartermaster had not merely been due to his clash with Sumner over accountability. Nor had Sumner just disagreed with Stuart's views on 'the practice of virtue.' They threatened him. 'Virtue' in the mind of Jeb Stuart, who toted his beaten little Episcopal *Book of Common Prayer* with him, whether through swollen streams or windswept prairie, stood in contrast to 'the elegant vices of city life.' He lost no love for the latter and the 'new-

ade city friends' to which he felt a couple of his southwest Virginia boyhood friends had succumbed.

Neither Sumner nor most of Stuart's peers understood how the wildest, best-riding, most brash and fearless, and arguably most formidable physical specimen among them could also desist from everything from alcoholic spirits to tobacco to cards and every form of wagering. But, aside from Sumner, most all the others liked and respected 'Beauty' Jeb Stuart even if they did not understand him.

Tom Munford, one of many who had bedeviled Major Thomas Jackson in his VMI section room and who now rode with Stuart, had asked Stuart about his disciplined practices around a lonely Nebraska campfire one summer night.

"Some thought I had renounced the cross when I went to West Point, a place usually considered at great variance with religion," Stuart told him. "But I rejoice to say I still have evidence of a Saviour's pardoning love."

When Munford pressed him on how he could forego the few mean worldly pleasures available during the long trackless months of frontier soldiering, Stuart replied, "When I entered West Point I knew many and strong temptations would beset my path, but I relied on Him whom to know is life everlasting to deliver me from temptation, and prayed God to guide me in the right way and teach me to walk as a Christian should; I have never for a moment hesitated to persevere; indeed, since coming to this far land I have been more than ever satisfied of the absolute importance of an acquaintance with Jesus our Lord."[22]

CHAPTER FOUR

GENERAL STUART'S CHRISTIAN TESTIMONY IS EVIDENCED IN HIS FEARLESSNESS AS A SOLDIER

"Christianity, true Christianity, steels a man. Because he knows the Almighty, he is bold to face the foe. No one is so bold as the man who is not afraid to die."[23] And that was exactly the kind of man that J.E.B. Stuart was. He would regularly remind the men under his command:

> Fear God, men, and you will have nothing else to fear.[24]

His military strategy was,

> ...when you are out numbered and it looks like you are overwhelmed, attack.[25]

"His boldness and his audacity were daunting, even among men who were not exactly unaccustomed to boldness and audacity. And yet he daunted them."[27]

General Stuart's Adjutant said that he:

> ...never saw him show any fear...The reason for that, you see, is not because Stuart was insane or had a few bricks shy of a full load, or whatever you want to call it. It was his trust in the Sovereignty of God."[28]

CHAPTER FIVE

GENERAL STUART'S CHRISTIAN TESTIMONY IS EVIDENCED IN THE FACT THAT HE ALWAYS FOUGHT FOR THE GLORY OF GOD

Dennis Wheeler begins his Theology of the Confederacy by stating that:

> When J.E.B. Stuart, 'Stonewall' Jackson, Robert E. Lee, and others took up arms to defend their people and their way of life against outside aggression, they were not merely acting out of self-interests, but were defending Christian civilization itself from those who had turned against it."[29]

Like many Southerners, J.E.B. Stuart felt "the sacredness of their cause."[30] J.E.B. believed that "defending home, hearth, and way of life"[31] would ensure victory over the North. It was his belief that God would see them through to triumph because of:

> His holy preference of a Christian people over a mercenary melange of Unitarians, Arminians, Jews, and Pope-followers.[32]

J.E.B. Stuart truly fought for the Glory of his God. Believing the cause to be just and holy J.E.B. Stuart devoted himself to it with an Ecclesiastes 9:10 zeal. He literally, "threw himself into the war with all his heart."[33]

As a soldier it was said that:

> Stuart 'possessed a Puritan streak nearly as wide as Jackson's.[34]

"He was the rare combination of the Puritan and the knight-errant."[35]

In his book Robert E. Lee and the Yankee Generals – A short Study in Contrasts, author Al Benson states the main contrast between the Yankee generals and Confederate generals Lee and Stuart was that Lee and Stuart were:

> ...humble believers who simply did their duty to their Saviour as they saw it."[36]

"Devotion to duty - duty to his God, duty to his country, was the ruling principle of his life."[37]

"Duty to God and his country were his watchwords."[38]

CHAPTER SIX

GENERAL STUART'S CHRISTIAN TESTIMONY IS EVIDENCED IN HIS FAITHFULNESS TO THE LOCAL CHURCH

As a child J.E.B. faithfully attended church services with his family.

J.E.B.'s father was "a fine singer" who would often sing solo and choir numbers in church.[39] J.E.B. and his brothers would also sing together during the church services.[40]

Stuart would remain faithful in his church attendance throughout his college and Army years. J.E.B. joined the Methodist Church when he was in college.[41] He faithfully attended Methodist services throughout his years at both Emory and Henry College and during his years as a Cadet at West Point.

J.E.B. especially enjoyed the sermons that his favorite teacher, Professor Sprole, delivered in the college chapel. He wrote to his cousin that:

> I shall miss his excellent sermons when I leave.[42]

While at West Point Stuart was known for ending his dates by going to church.[43]

From 1857-1861, while stationed at Fort Riley, Kansas, then Lieutenant and Mrs. Stuart faithfully attended the Episcopal Church of the Covenant in Junction City. Mrs. Stuart played the piano for all of the church's services and the congregation presented the couple with a silver tea set upon their departure in 1861.[44]

In 1859 Stuart officially transferred his membership to the Episcopal Church. He shared his reasons for changing church membership with Major McClellan:

> He found that a majority of the chaplains in the United States Army at that time were Episcopalian divines, and he considered that his opportunities for Christian fellowship and church privileges would be increased by the change.[45]

When the Stuart family moved back to Virginia at the beginning of the War for Southern Independence J.E.B.'s main criteria in choosing a family home was the closeness of the house to the church. J.E.B. wrote the following to his wife:

> I am very much in favor of Charlottesville as a home...The society is excellent and every variety of the Episcopal Church is near the location I would select.[46]

Even through the hardships of war General Stuart's attendance to religious services did not diminish. When in Richmond General Stuart would attend the old St. Paul's Church.[47] Stuart was also reported to have attended Saint James Church.[48]

In April of 1863 Stuart wrote his wife telling her how he had taken time off from his regular military duties one Friday evening to attend the services of a Fredericksburg church. He reported that he "heard a fine sermon to a crowded congregation."[49]

Beginning in 1862 religious rivals began to sweep through the Southern army camps. General Stuart was, "...noted for his participation in the services..."[50]

The papers of the Southern Historical Society note that J.E.B. was, "a deeply interested listener" [51] who faithfully attended the meetings of the Army Chaplains' Association.

Stuart would often plan religious services and other religious activities for his men. Rev. J. William Jones, the head of the Army of Northern Virginia's Chaplain's Corps, reported that General Stuart would often come to him for advice as he planned the services.[52]

CHAPTER SEVEN

GENERAL STUART'S CHRISTIAN TESTIMONY IS EVIDENCED IN HIS EFFORTS TO SEEK THE CONVERSION OF OTHERS

The Preface to Mary Williamson's The Life of J.E.B. Stuart states that General Stuart:

> ...was a powerful witness for Jesus Christ to countless soldiers who served in the War Between the States.[53]

Major H.B. McClellan said that General Stuart was:

> ...careful, as far as possible, to provide chaplains for all of his regiments, and encouraged the holding of religious meetings.[54]

General Stuart went to great efforts to ensure that Bibles, gospel tracts, and other bible study materials were readily available to his men. He even paid for the printing and distribution of these materials himself. In November of 1863 he sent a letter to the Presbyterian missionary agency requesting materials. He wrote:

> Please find enclosed $36 which I wish expended for detached portions of Scriptures - the Gospels preferred - which I wish to distribute among my friends in the ranks.[55]

When, the printing of Bibles and other literature became scarce in the South, General Stuart sent Dr. Moses Hoge, a Presbyterian minister, across the ocean on a special assignment to purchase Bibles and tracts in England. Stuart gave Dr. Hoge a personal check to use as payment for the materials. The check was never cashed because the London Bible Society donated the Bibles and other literature to the Confederate Government for distribution to the soldiers. The check is still in the possession of Dr. Hoge's descendants.[56]

However, J.E.B.'s "soul-winning" efforts were not limited to the distribution of Bibles and literature. He also took a personal interest in the salvation of individual men and sought earnestly to win them. He was especially burdened for the salvation of fellow-General Elisha Paxton. "Stonewall" Jackson reported that one day General Stuart rode into his camp just to tell him that, "we must be about getting Bull Paxton saved."[57]

In fact, J.E.B. Stuart may have even been the last person to share the gospel with the famous abolitionist terrorist John Brown.[58]

In 1859, when John Brown launched his infamous attack on Harper's Ferry then Lieutenant Stuart just happened to be in the area attending a Layman's Convention of the Episcopal Church.[59] Then Lieutenant-Colonel Robert E. Lee, who was also attending the convention, was called to service to capture Brown and he took Stuart along to serve as his Aide.[60]

It was Stuart who led the actual charge of Marines into the building where John Brown and his hostages were holed-up and thus Lieutenant Stuart was the first person to make contact with John Brown. Stuart pled with Brown from the scriptures, reminding him that "The wages of sin is death." and asked him to repent and call on the Saviour.[61]

J.E.B. Stuart was also an active church planter.

While stationed at Fort Riley, Kansas, then Lieutenant Stuart raised the funds and led in the construction of the Episcopal Church of the Covenant in Junction City.[62]

Later, wishing to see the gospel preached to his old neighbors and acquaintances, Stuart wrote the following letter to his mother, offering to purchase land and donate money toward the construction of a church:

> I wish to devote one hundred dollars to the purchase of a comfortable log church near our place, because in all my observation I believe that one is more needed in that neighborhood than any other that I know of... If you will join me with a like amount from two or three others interested we will build a very respectable *free* church...What will you take for the South half of your plantation? I want to buy it.[63]

CHAPTER EIGHT

GENERAL STUART'S CHRISTIAN TESTIMONY IS EVIDENCED IN HIS FAITHFULNESS TO THE KING JAMES BIBLE AND PRAYER

J.E.B. Stuart was noted by all who knew him as a man who was faithful in personal devotions, Bible reading, and in both public and private prayer.[64]

Biographer Burke Davis notes that each morning during the War for Southern Independence General Stuart, "rose before day to read the Bible by firelight."[65]

Stuart would honestly testify that even during the most stressful periods of the war his prayer book "has not been neglected."[66] In fact, it was said that Stuart was "inseparable from his Prayer Book."[67] Why once, when on frontier duty in Texas, Stuart nearly risked his own life to save his prayer book from a prairie fire:

> The portmanteau which contained my clothing was burnt with its contents except a portfolio containing my paper and a prayer book which I rescued narrowly, but not without the mark of the fire.[68]

Mr. Channing, in whose home Stuart's temporary Command Headquarters was established, noted the following about the General:

> ...his bible and prayer book were often objects of his attention and his conduct while with me was as exemplary as a Christian's could have been.[69]

It was said that his Aides would often catch, "glimpses of him in his tent late at night, his work completed, head in his arms at his desk, his powerful shoulders quaking with grief, little Flora's photograph and the same old prayer book, opened beneath him."[70]

General Stuart was often reported to:

> ...participate in the prayer meetings that occupied the camps during the great revivals that swept through the Confederate Armies.[71]

Even in the heat of the battle, General Stuart, like "Stonewall," would stop to pray.[72] He once wrote to his brother that:

> With me, no moment of the battle is ever too momentous for prayer.[73]

CHAPTER NINE

GENERAL STUART'S CHRISTIAN TESTIMONY IS EVIDENCED IN THE WAY HE LIVED THE SCRIPTURE

J.E.B. Stuart's "life verse" was Proverbs 17:22, *"A merry heart doeth good like a medicine: but a broken spirit drieth the bones."* This is why J.E.B. Stuart was always laughing and why he always did his best to make others laugh.[74]

General Stuart hosted several parties during the war and he was always the life of every party that he attended. He always maintained a "merry heart" and he always worked hard at making everyone around him equally "merry" in their heart.[75]

Nearly every biography of the General makes much of the fact that he was a very "jovial" person. Yet sadly very few biographers take the time to explain why the General worked so hard at it. Jest and laughter, though playful, were not entered into lightly. They were but one of many ways in which J.E.B. Stuart strove in his daily life to live the scripture.

This is because J.E.B. Stuart did not just think of the Bible as a book to be read and admired. It was **The Book** upon which he based his life and conversation.[76]

On the following pages are a listing of just a few of the verses that General Stuart had underscored in his Bible with accompanying examples of how he applied the passages in his daily life.

- **Proverbs 19:15, "*Slothfulness casteth into a deep sleep; and an idle soul shall suffer hunger.*"**

J.E.B. was often heard to say, "I like to be doing something all the time."[77]

- **Proverbs 22:1, "*A good name is rather to be chosen than great riches.*"**

J.E.B. wrote the following to his wife in April of 1863 regarding the selection of a name for their expected child:

> If a boy, I wish him to be called Jon Pelham Stuart. I have thought of it much—it is my choice. His record is complete and it is spotless. It is noble. His family was the very best. His character was pure, his disposition as sweet and innocent as our own little Flora's.[78]

- **Proverbs 22:7, "*the borrower is servant to the lender.*"**

J.E.B. wrote the following to his father while serving as a Cadet at West Point:

> Your kind letter arrived yesterday. I thank you very much for the remittance you were pleased to make me... You need not send me any more as the sum you sent will last me till next June. I will endeavor to appreciate your kind admonition in regard to debt to my utmost. It is bad enough for a young man of fortune when setting out in life to become involved and encumbered by a load of debt, but how much worse is it for one without fortune when about to launch into life to find at the first step, debt.[79]

- **Ecclesiastes 9:10, *"Whatsoever thy hand findeth to do, do it with thy might."***

It was said of J.E.B. Stuart that, "He always worked hard at anything."[80]

- **Luke 6:31, *"And as ye would that men should do to you, do ye also to them likewise."***

All who knew the General agreed that, "Stuart treated his men as he desired to be treated,"[81]

- **Luke 17: 9-10, *"Doth he thank that servant because he did the things that were commanded him? I trow not. So likewise ye, when ye shall have done all those things which are commanded you, say, We are unprofitable servants: we have done that which was our duty to do."***

J.E.B. Wrote the following to one of his teachers while he was a cadet at West Point:

> I take no credit whatever to myself for my success, for you know a man deserves no praise for doing what he is obliged to do.[82]

- **Acts 10:34, *"God is no respecter of persons."***

It was said of General Stuart that:

> He was the most approachable of generals, and jested with the private soldiers as jovially as if he had been one of them.[83]

- **Romans 13:7, "Render therefore to all their dues: tribute to whom tribute is due; custom to whom custom; fear to whom fear; honour to whom honour."**

Stuart was free with praise of officers and men.[84]

- **James 3:2, "If any man offend not...the same is a perfect man"**

J.E.B. Stuart was known for his "interesting" wardrobe. Many historians have imagined that Stuart wore so many "fancies" because he was a show-off. Nothing could be further from the truth. The fancy hat, the sash, the golden spurs, and every other do-dad that Stuart wore he put on only because they were gifts from neighbors and influential members of society.

When J.E.B. Stuart went to town he wore everything that anyone had ever given him just in case they would happen to see him. He did not want for any of his neighbors to be offended should they see him and he was not wearing their gift.[85]

Since combat photography as we know it would not be invented until the Spanish-American War, most of the photographs taken during the War Between the States were taken in town, at headquarters, and occasionally in camp – but almost never in battle. So nearly all of the wartime photographs of Stuart were taken when he was in town and dressed up for the sake of his friends and neighbors. The one and only known photograph to be taken of General Stuart in combat shows him to be dressed very plainly. He was wearing a simple pair of grey trousers, a plaid flannel shirt, his sword, and a pistol holster.

CHAPTER TEN

GENERAL STUART'S CHRISTIAN TESTIMONY IS EVIDENCED IN THAT HE WAS A MAN WITHOUT VICE

In his famous biography of "Stonewall" Jackson, historian John Dwyer notes that:

> Stuart's personal purity and piety were well known in the land.[86]

After having spent most of the war in very close quarters with General Stuart, Major H. B. McClellan reported that:

> No stain of vice or immorality was ever found upon him.[87]

J.E.B. Stuart never drank intoxicating beverages[88] and he never used strong stimulants.[89] "In fact, he promised his mother at the age of twelve that he would never drink whiskey or alcohol, and he kept his promise."[90]

At the beginning of the war J.E.B. even made his wife's cousin promise him that:

> If I am ever wounded, don't let them give me any whisky or brandy. I promised my mother when I was twelve that I would never touch it.[91]

After the Battle of Yellow Tavern, as General Stuart was being treated for the mortal wound which he had received during the day's battle, Dr. Fontaine "urged him to take some whiskey as a stimulant."[92] But General Stuart refused saying, "I've never tasted it in my life..."[93]

And J.E.B. Stuart was at all times faithful to his wife. He wrote at least one letter to his wife for every day of their married life.[94] He would often express his love and devotion to her in such terms as:

> My darling if you could know—(and I think you ought) how true I am to you and how centered in you is my every hope—and dream of earthly bliss, you would never listen to the idle twaddle of those who knowing how we love each other amuse themselves telling such outlandish fare as the beard story to see how you would stand it.[95]

"There were sometimes rumors started by his enemies and those who coveted his fame that Stuart was too careless in his dealing with women. These are all without foundation and fact. Every one of his men, who were on the staff and closest to him, were with him all the time, and they were offended more than he was at the constant implications. All those close to him testified unanimously that Stuart was always careful to avoid trespassing the bounds of strict propriety in all of his relationships with women. He, like Robert E. Lee, did enjoy the social company of women. Robert E. Lee always said that, and always made a point of telling Mrs. Lee about it, and Stuart did the same. He would fill his letters with the names of any ladies he had conversed with... there was nothing inappropriate... The love of his life was his wife, and that was plain to everyone."[96]

"There was no woman who, in General Stuart's eyes, could compare with his wife, and he was never happier than when with her and his children."[97]

In fact, there were:

> ...few things that Stuart despised more than marital infidelity. He hated it. He once captured a Union soldier's trunk and when they opened it, they found

some letters. There were some loving letters from this man's wife, but right beside those letters were some other letters, obscene letters from a mistress he had taken up with in the Army. He looked at both letters and it was clear his wife did not know about the mistress. So Stuart decided he would make her acquainted with this woman. He boxed up all the letters and had a messenger take the letters to this man's wife."[98]

When writing of this incident in his official report to General Lee, Stuart's brother-in-law, John Eston Cooke, wrote, with some understatement, "There will be a fuss in that family."[99]

After the war many of his soldiers reported that they had, "never heard him curse or swear in battle."[100]

The official Confederate Military History concluded its report on General Stuart by recording that, he:

> ...indulged in none of the vices supposed to be habitual with soldiers, was never profane, and even abstained from card-playing. He was a faithful husband and father, and altogether one of the purest of men, as well as the bravest."[101]

The 19th century biographer Mary Williamson summarized J.E.B. Stuarts Christian Character by writing that:

> His gallantry, boldness, and joyful spirit, coupled with his high Christian virtues, caused all who came in contact with him not only to love but to respect and admire him.[102]

CHAPTER ELEVEN

GENERAL STUART'S CHRISTIAN TESTIMONY IS EVIDENCED IN HIS PERSONAL LETTERS

In her book on General Stuart, Adelle Mitchell writes:

> From his mother Jeb Stuart inherited a love of all that was beautiful in nature and under her influence he developed the faith in God that is so evident in many of his letters.[103]

It was my privilege to receive by insured currier some 300 of these letters which the Stuart family entrusted to me for a one-month period. Included in the package, General Stuart's great grandson, Colonel J.E.B. Stuart IV, wrote the following in regard to the letters:

> As you read through these letters, there are several attributes of General Stuart that will become readily apparent; a deep belief in the Supreme Being and the ascribing of his success to Divine Providence.[104]

The letters were dated throughout a ten-year period from 1853 to 1863. The following are excerpts from some of those letters. Each • symbol represents a citation from a different or separate letter.

1853:

- Dear Pa, In making the selection I will rely upon the guidance of Him whose judgment cannot err, for it "is not with man that walketh to direct his steps.

- From the first I prayed to God to be my guide...

1855:

- Mr. Thompson, These dispensations of an all wise providence must be experienced by all. His will not mine be done.

1857:

- Pray for me and ask Mr. Goodwin to pray for the success of our arms.

1861:

- My Darling Wife, I put you in God's holy keeping.
- My Darling Wife, Put your trust in God.
- My Dear Wife, We must nerve our hearts for the trial with a firm reliance on God...let me hear her noble words of encouragement and faith.
- My Darling Wife, May God bless you, Dearest.
- My Darling, let us trust in the Good God, who has blessed us so much, to spare our child to us, but if it should please him to take her from us let us bear it with Christian fortitude and resignation.
- I hope to do my duty with a firm reliance on Divine Aid to uphold me.

1862:

- The next summer will probably be the most eventful in a century. We must nerve our hearts for the trial with a firm reliance on God.
- Let us trust in the good God who has blessed us so much, that he will spare our child to us, but if it should please Him to take her from us, let us bear it with Christian fortitude and resignation.

- She is better off, I know... She is up in Heaven where she will still pray for her Pa and look down upon him in the day of battle.

- My Dear <u>Dear</u> Lily: Tell our friends everywhere to pray for us...Keep a prayerful spirit.

1863

- My Darling One, God has preserved me through another conflict and crowned us with victory.

- My Dear Cousin: ...the sincere prayer that this sad affliction may be sanctified to our eternal welfare...bow in submission to the decree of an all-wise God and say in our humble supplications "<u>Thy</u> <u>Will</u> <u>be</u> <u>Done</u>"

- My Darling Wife: God has spared me through another bloody battle, and blessed with victory our arms.

- My Darling Wife: Scarcely a moment to write. God has spared my life and blessed us with success thus far.

- Major Von Borcke is better. I do pray he may get well.

- My Darling Wife: Upon the eve of another battle I write today to say God has mercifully spared me through many dangers and bloody fields.

- How much better to have your husband I his grave after a career true to every duty and every responsibility, to you, his country, and his God, than inglorious existence – a living shame to you and to his children.

- God has spared me through another bloody battle and given us the victory yesterday and the day before.

- I write to say God has mercifully spared me through many dangers and bloody fields. My cavalry has nobly sustained its reputation, and done better and harder fighting than it ever has since the war. Pray, without ceasing, that God will grant us the victory.

- Flora: ...I was never in greater personal danger and men and horses fell around me like tenpins, but thanks to God to whom I looked for protection, neither myself no my horse was touched.

- I go forth into the uncertain future. My saber will not leave my hand for months. I am sustained in the hour of peril by the consciousness of right, and upheld by the same Almighty hand, which has thus far covered my head in the day of battle, and in whom I put my trust.

Clearly J.E.B. Stuart was not hesitant to declare his faith on the written page.

One letter in particular, written during his first year at the Military Academy to some friends at Emory and Henry College, very clearly exhibits the faith that J.E.B. Stuart had in the Lord Jesus Christ. Stuart wrote:

> I expect that you as well as all of my old friends about Emory have come to the conclusion that I have renounced the cross, since I came to this place, usually considered at so great a variance with religion. But I rejoice to say I still have evidence of a Savior's pardoning love, and when I came here, I had reason to expect that many and strong temptations would beset my path, but I relied on Him who to know is life everlasting, to deliver me from temptation, and prayed God to guide me in the right way and to teach me to walk as a Christian should. I have never for a moment hesitated to persevere. Indeed, since I came here, I have been more than ever satisfied of the absolute importance of an acquaintance with the Lord.[105]

CHAPTER TWELVE

GENERAL STUART'S CHRISTIAN TESTIMONY IS EVIDENCED IN HIS MILITARY REPORTS

Just as General Stuart's Christian faith was evident in the written pages of his personal letters, it is also clearly evident on the written pages of his military orders and reports. As he wrote his reports he was always "ever careful to attribute the success and blessing he had to the Lord's goodness."[106]

General Stuart's reports regularly contained such phrases as:

> "Blessed be God that giveth us the victory."[107]
>
> "Pray, without ceasing, that God will grant us the victory."[108]
>
> "May God grant us victory."[109]

In one report, he gives the following assessment of a Major Norman Fitzhugh:

> He is honest, capable, and a devoted Christian.[110]

In a report to General Isaac Trimble he writes:

> Yours of September 26th did not reach me till after church yesterday.[111]

Stuart once closed his report to General Lee with:

> Believing that the hand of God was clearly manifest in the signal deliverance of my command from danger and

the crowning success attending it, I ascribe to Him the praise, the honour and the glory.[112]

In a General Order issued to his troops after Brandy Station, General Stuart writes:

> With an abiding faith in the God of our fathers...your success will continue.[113]

CHAPTER THIRTEEN

GENERAL STUART'S CHRISTIAN TESTIMONY IS EVIDENCED IN HIS PERSONAL POETRY

The League of the South Lecture Series tape on the life of General Stuart begins by stating that:

> ...among other things, General Stuart was known for his poetry. Very, very BAD poetry.[114]

J.E.B. Stuart's attempts at poetry may not have won him any literary prizes. But they do demonstrate that he was a man of intense faith.

The Stuart Family was kind enough to entrust to me for a brief period General Stuart's personal poetry book which they had shipped to me by an insured currier. Because of General Stuart's poor handwriting, coupled with the fact that I am almost entirely used to reading typed pages rather than handwritten ones, I found myself unable to read more than ¾ of the book's contents. Much of what I could read had obviously been written by a man of Christian faith.

One of my favorites was:

> Shivering, 'midst the darkness,
> Christian men are found,
> There devoutly kneeling
> On the frozen ground -
> Pleading for their country,
> In its hour of woe -
> For its soldiers marching
> Shoeless through the snow.

This one was written in both his poetry book and again on the leaf of his prayer book:

> O God, where'er my footsteps stray
> On prairies far or battles dim
> Still keep them in thy holy way.
> And cleanse my soul from ev'ry sin.
>
> Lord! When the hour of death shall come
> O grant that I may have a home
> In thy abode of endless peace.

Here are some very short excerpts from much longer poems:

- *Devotion to the cause of truth may heavenly light upon thy path serenely glory shed*

- *May the hand of Heaven His blessing on thy labor send.*

- *I'll hang my harp on a willow tree and hushed will be its strain*

- *Lingering in the smile of God*

- *Him whose blood He spilt*

- *She is going to the Lord of purest delight*

Sometimes Stuart would write humorous poems with biblical themes. One such example was a poem he entitled *My Beard Flourishes Like the Gourd of Jonah*:

> And long may it wave
> For I ne'er will shave
> While My Flora approves
> Still to grow it behooves
> And 'nary a hair'
> From it will I spare.[115]

CHAPTER FOURTEEN

GENERAL STUART'S CHRISTIAN TESTIMONY IS EVIDENCED IN THE ACCOUNTS OF HIS HAVING DIED WITH A FULL ASSURANCE OF HIS CHRISTIAN FAITH

As J.E.B. Stuart lay mortally wounded, he responded to someone who told him that he would be all right by saying:

> Well I don't know how this will turn out, but if its God's will that I should die I am ready.[116]

A little later, as his men began to retreat, he cried out to them:

> Go back! go back and do your duty as I have done, and our country will be safe. Go back! go back! I had rather die than be whipped.[117]

Later he would cry out to them again:

> God grant that you may be successful.[118]

Then turning his head aside, he sighed and told his aide:

> But I must be prepared for another world.[119]

The next day, President Jefferson Davis came and visited him. He said, "General, how do you feel?" Stuart looked at him and said:

> Well, easy, but willing to die, if God and my country think I have fulfilled my destiny and done my duty.[120]

During the afternoon, on one of Dr. Brewer's visits, Stuart asked:

> How long can I live, Charles? Can I last through the night?[121]

"I'm afraid the end is near,"[122] Brewer said.

Stuart nodded and said:

> I am resigned, if it be God's will. I would like to see my wife. But God's will be done.[123]

His Pastor, Dr. Peterkin, visited him, and prayed with him. He requested Dr. Peterkin to sing the hymn *Rock of Ages*, and joined in the singing of the hymn.[124]

"His worldly matters closed, the eternal interest of his soul engaged his mind. Turning to his pastor, he joined with him in prayer."[125]

Then Stuart turned to his physician, Dr. Brewer, and said:

> I'm going fast now. God's will be done...[126]

"He was gone. The pulse was still."[127] As he "passed through the valley of the Shadow of Death"[128] his well worn New Testament came from his pocket.[129] "It was twenty-two minutes before eight,"[130] General Stuart was with the Lord.[131]

He died on the 12th of May, 1864.[132] His dying words were from the second stanza of the beloved hymn *Rock of Ages Cleft for Me*. The General whispered:

> In my hand no price I bring, simply to thy cross I cling.[133]

CHAPTER FIFTEEN

GENERAL STUART'S CHRISTIAN TESTIMONY IS EVIDENCED IN THE EULOGIES GIVEN AFTER HIS DEATH

J.E.B.'s Brother-in-Law, John Esten Cooke, issued the following statement immediately after the death of General Stuart:

> ...his life had been one of earnest devotion to the cause in which he believed...his last hours were tranquil, his confidence in the mercy of heaven unfailing.[134]

General Robert E. Lee wrote the following to the men of the Confederate Cavalry shortly after General Stuart's death:

> To military capacity of a high order, General Stuart added the brighter graces of a pure life guided and sustained by the Christian's faith and hope.[135]

The Rev. J. William Jones offered the following memorial to General Stuart:

> Stuart was an humble and earnest Christian who took Christ as his personal Saviour, lived a stainless life, and died a triumphant death.[136]

The Yankee General Oliver Howard wrote a very complimentary eulogy to his opponent, General Stuart:

> J. E. B. Stuart was cut out for a cavalry leader.... Christian in thought and temperate by habit, no man could ride faster, endure more hardships, make a livelier

charge, or be more hearty and cheerful while so engaged.[137]

Michael McHugh wrote the following Poem in tribute to General Stuart:

> The trumpet call was heard by some,
> Who left the comforts of their home,
> To war for Southern liberty,
> To fight for home and family.
>
> "Jeb" Stuart was one such man,
> He died and fought for his native land,
> A pure and noble night was he,
> Doing his utmost for God, honor, and dignity.
>
> -- Michael J. McHugh[138]

In a post-war memorial service for General Stuart The Reverend J. Steven Wilkins noted that:

> The thing that dominated Jeb Stuart was his love for Christ. As it is with all men, the most important ingredient in Stuart's character was his faith. That foundation was the basis for all he was and all that he did. Biblical Christianity; he trusted implicitly in God and committed himself, his family and his men to the care and keeping of the great Saviour of mankind.[139]

Reverend Thompson noted that:

> His letters, his remembered conversations and even his official papers make it plain that his religion was an active force in everything he did, and he had a very simple and earnest faith in the wisdom and goodness of God.[140]

Speaking to a packed house during a memorial service at the Virginia House of Delegates Stuart's Aide, Major H.B. McClellan, said of General Stuart:

> ...He had this light and joyous nature constituted the controlling feature of Stuart's character, he would never have achieved greatness. The temptations of youth would probably have carried him away into excesses which would have ruined his usefulness. But, as I have already said, in his boyhood he professed the religion of Christ, and ever afterward maintained a consistent Christian character. He was absolutely pure and temperate in his personal habits. I have heard him say repeatedly, never had one drop of spirituous liquor of any kind passed his lips, and that he had not even tasted wine except at the sacramental table.
>
> His reliance upon an overruling Providence was simple and complete.
>
> ...he reverently recognizes the fact that the disposal of his life is in the hands of the Supreme Power.
>
> ...In every great success which crowned his arms in after days, he gives thanks to the kind Providence which has guided and protected him through a thousand dangers.[141]

One of the soldiers who had fought under Stuart's direct command said that:

> He trusted God implicitly.[142]

One of Stuart's cousins noted that:

> He saw the things that God provided as manifestations of God's goodness.[143]

Captain R. E. Frayser gave the following tribute to General Stuart:

> I have known him to lie on the ground, and exposed to all kinds of weather, giving as a reason that he did not wish to fare more comfortably than his men.
>
> There was something about Stuart that drew you to him. He was courageous. He was audacious in his boldness. He was a man of strict integrity, a godly Christian man. He was a man of great principles.[144]

An obituary noted that:

> Stuart was a true man of faith for he trusted God to shepherd him wisely and mercifully.[145]

The Confederate Veteran Magazine reported that:

> Stuart was a deeply religious man and a faithful husband.[146]

CHAPTER SIXTEEN

IN MY HAND NO PRICE I BRING

As was noted in chapter fourteen, General Stuart's dying words were:

> In my hand no price I bring, simply to thy cross I cling.[147]

As he crossed from time into eternity, General Stuart knew that he needn't bring any payment. He wasn't expecting to enter Heaven on the merits of his good works, his clean life, church membership, water baptism, money he had given to the church, the fact that he was a veteran, or any other human work or device. His trust was completely and wholly in the fact that Jesus Christ had died on the cross and shed His own blood to pay the price in full.

General Stuart did not expect to enter Heaven on his own merits. Rather, he expected to enter Heaven because of the merits of Jesus Christ.

General Stuart realized that:

> For by grace are ye saved through faith; and that not of yourselves: it is the gift of God: Not of works, lest any man should boast.[148]

In my hand no price I bring, simply to thy cross I cling.

Whats in your hand? In what are you trusting for eternal salvation? Hopefully, just like General Stuart, you are trusting in absolutely nothing except for Christ's death on the cross.

Are you 100% sure that you will meet General Stuart in Heaven one day? You can be. I John 5:13 tells us:

> These things have I written unto you that believe on the name of the Son of God; that ye may know that ye have eternal life, and that ye may believe on the name of the Son of God.

FIRST: YOU MUST ACCEPT THAT YOU ARE A SINNER.

"For all have sinned and come short of the glory of God"
-- Romans 3:23

No one is perfect, no one has lived up to God's perfect standard.

SECOND: YOU MUST ACCEPT THAT AS A SINNER YOU OWE A PENALTY.

"For the wages of sin is death…." -- Romans 6:23

This death is described in the Bible as the "second death," the Lake of Fire.

"Death and hell were cast into the lake of fire. This is the second death" -- Revelation 20:14

In order for us to pay the debt we owe ourselves, we would have to spend all eternity in the Lake of Fire (Hell).

THIRD: YOU MUST ACCEPT THAT JESUS CHRIST HAS ALREADY PAID YOUR SIN DEBT.

"But God commendeth his love toward us, in that, while we were yet sinners, Christ died for us" -- Romans 5:8

Jesus was not a sinner, yet the Bible teaches that God took all of our sins and placed them upon Him:

"For he hath made him to be sin for us, who knew no sin; that we might be made the righteousness of God in him"
-- 2 Corinthians 5:21

While Jesus was on the cross, bearing our sins in His body, God punished Him in our place to pay the debt that we owe.

FOURTH: YOU MUST ACCEPT BY FAITH WHAT JESUS HAS DONE FOR YOU.

"He that believeth on the Son hath everlasting life, and he that believeth not the Son shall not see life; but the wrath of God abideth on him" (John 3:36).

Dear friend, if you have not already done so, why not call on Jesus right now and trust Him to save you.

"For whosoever shall call upon the name of the Lord shall be saved." -- Romans 10:13

To talk to someone about becoming a Christian, or for help as you grow in your Christian life do not hesitate to E-mail me: **Dr.DeVries@bibleschool.edu**

CHAPTER SIXTEEN

A GODLY LEGACY

"A good man leaveth an inheritance to his children's children." -- Proverbs 13:22

Just before his death, General Stuart penned these words of instruction to his wife:

> When I am gone train up my boy in the footsteps of his father and tell him never to falter in implicit faith in Divine Providence.[149]

As a postscript for this book I called J.E.B. Stuart IV one afternoon and asked him some questions about his own Christian faith and that of his father, his grandfather, his children, and his grandchildren. Colonel Stuart assured me that the Christian Faith has continued in the Stuart family through the present day.

J.E.B. II grew up in the Episcopal Church and was educated in the church's school. He remained faithful in his church attendance and in working in the church throughout his adult life.

J.E.B. III received Christ as his Saviour as a very young man. As an adult he moved to New York City where he became an active member of the Dutch Reformed Church.

J.E.B IV was raised in the Dutch Reformed Church. He professed faith and became active in church life while serving as a 1st Lieutenant in the United States Army. He and his wife are active members of the St. James' Episcopal Church in Richmond, Virginia

JEB V serves as an elder in the Grace Episcopal Church in Goochland, Virginia.

JEB VI is, at the time of this writing, 14-years old. His baptism at St. James' Church was one of the highest attended services in the recent history of the church. He is active in the teen and youth programs of the Grace Episcopal Church where he serves as an Acolyte and assists the Pastor during the services.[150]

END NOTES

1- *The Life of J.E.B. Stuart*, Mary L. Williamson, Christian Liberty Press, p. 1
2- *The Life of J.E.B. Stuart*, Mary L. Williamson, Christian Liberty Press, p. 1
3- *Jeb Stuart The Last Cavalier*, Burke Davis, Burford Books, Short Hills, New Jersey, 1957, p. 17
4- *Jeb Stuart The Last Cavalier*, Burke Davis, Burford Books, Short Hills, New Jersey, 1957, p. 17
5- *Jeb Stuart The Last Cavalier*, Burke Davis, Burford Books, Short Hills, New Jersey, 1957, p. 18
6- *Boy in the Saddle*, Gertrude Winders, Howard W. Sams & Co., Inc., New York, 1959, p. 139
7- *Boy in the Saddle*, Gertrude Winders, Howard W. Sams & Co., Inc., New York, 1959, p. 40
8- *The Life of General J.E.B. Stuart*, J. Steven Wilkins, Birmingham, Alabama
9- *The Life of General J.E.B. Stuart*, J. Steven Wilkins, Birmingham, Alabama
10- *The Life of General J.E.B. Stuart*, J. Steven Wilkins, Birmingham, Alabama
11- *The Life of General J.E.B. Stuart*, J. Steven Wilkins, Birmingham, Alabama
12- *The Letters of J.E.B. Stuart* – Courtesy of the Stuart Family
13- *The Life of J.E.B. Stuart*, Mary L. Williamson, Christian Liberty Press, pg. 4
14- *Stonewall*, John Dwyer, Broadman & Holman, Nashville, Tenn., 1998, p. 333
15- *Jeb Stuart The Last Cavalier*, Burke Davis, Burford Books, Short Hills, New Jersey, 1957, p. 22-23
16- *Stonewall*, John Dwyer, Broadman & Holman, Nashville, Tenn., 1998, p. 333
17- *The Life of General J.E.B. Stuart*, J. Steven Wilkins, Birmingham, Alabama
18- *The Life of J.E.B. Stuart*, Mary L. Williamson, Christian Liberty Press, pg. 5
19- *Stonewall*, John Dwyer, Broadman & Holman, Nashville, Tenn., 1998, p. 307

20- *The Life of J.E.B. Stuart*, Mary L. Williamson, Christian Liberty Press, pg. 11
21- *Stonewall*, John Dwyer, Broadman & Holman, Nashville, Tenn., 1998, p. 615
22- *Stonewall*, John Dwyer, Broadman & Holman, Nashville, Tenn., 1998, p. 306
23- *The Life of General J.E.B. Stuart*, J. Steven Wilkins, Birmingham, Alabama
24- *The Life of General J.E.B. Stuart*, J. Steven Wilkins, Birmingham, Alabama
25- *The Life of General J.E.B. Stuart*, J. Steven Wilkins, Birmingham, Alabama
26- *The Life of General J.E.B. Stuart*, J. Steven Wilkins, Birmingham, Alabama
27- *The Life of General J.E.B. Stuart*, J. Steven Wilkins, Birmingham, Alabama
28- *The Life of General J.E.B. Stuart*, J. Steven Wilkins, Birmingham, Alabama
29- http://dennisw.home.mindspring.com
30- *Stonewall*, John Dwyer, Broadman & Holman, Nashville, Tenn., 1998, p. 404
31- *Stonewall*, John Dwyer, Broadman & Holman, Nashville, Tenn., 1998, p. 404
32- *Stonewall*, John Dwyer, Broadman & Holman, Nashville, Tenn., 1998, p. 404
33- *Boy in the Saddle*, Gertrude Winders, Howard W. Sams & Co., Inc., New York, 1959, p. 179
34- *Stonewall*, John Dwyer, Broadman & Holman, Nashville, Tenn., 1998, p. 404
35- *The Life of J.E.B. Stuart*, Mary L. Williamson, Christian Liberty Press, pg. 97
36- http://www.patriotist.com/abarch/ab20010122.htm
37- Major H. B. McClellan, October 27, 1880, Virginia House of Delegates
38- *The Life of J.E.B. Stuart*, Mary L. Williamson, Christian Liberty Press, pg. 67
39- *Boy in the Saddle*, Gertrude Winders, Howard W. Sams & Co., Inc., New York, 1959, p. 139
40- *Boy in the Saddle*, Gertrude Winders, Howard W. Sams & Co., Inc., New York, 1959, p. 40
41- *The Life and Campaigns of Major-General J.E.B. Stuart*, H.B. McClellan, Chapter 1

42- *The Letters of J.E.B. Stuart* – Courtesy of the Stuart Family
43- *Major General James E. B. Stuart,* Adelle H. Mitchell, p.85
44- *Major General James E. B. Stuart,* Adelle H. Mitchell, p. 410
45- *The Life and Campaigns of Major-General J.E.B. Stuart*, H.B. McClellan, Chapter 1
46- *Major General James E. B. Stuart,* Adelle H. Mitchell, p. 363
47- *Jeb Stuart The Last Cavalier*, Burke Davis, Burford Books, Short Hills, New Jersey, 1957, p. 90
48- *Jeb Stuart The Last Cavalier*, Burke Davis, Burford Books, Short Hills, New Jersey, 1957, p. 307
49- *The Letters of J.E.B. Stuart* – Courtesy of the Stuart Family
50- *Jeb Stuart The Last Cavalier*, Burke Davis, Burford Books, Short Hills, New Jersey, 1957, p. 240
51- *Southern Historical Society Papers Volume VII - No 2*, February 1878
52- *The Life of J.E.B. Stuart*, Mary L. Williamson, Christian Liberty Press, pg. 53
53- *The Life of J.E.B. Stuart*, Mary L. Williamson, Christian Liberty Press, pg. iii
54- Major H. B. McClellan, October 27, 1880, Virginia House of Delegates
55- *Major General James E. B. Stuart,* Adelle H. Mitchell, p.355-356
56- *Major General James E. B. Stuart,* Adelle H. Mitchell, p. 426
57- *Stonewall*, John Dwyer, Broadman & Holman, Nashville, Tenn., 1998, p. 551
58- *Jeb Stuart The Last Cavalier*, Burke Davis, Burford Books, Short Hills, New Jersey, 1957, p. 14
59- http://www.civilwarhome.com/stuartjohnbrown.htm
60- http://www.civilwarhome.com/stuartjohnbrown.htm
61- *Jeb Stuart The Last Cavalier*, Burke Davis, Burford Books, Short Hills, New Jersey, 1957, p.14
62- *Major General James E. B. Stuart,* Adelle H. Mitchell, p. 410
63- *Jeb Stuart The Last Cavalier*, Burke Davis, Burford Books, Short Hills, New Jersey, 1957, p. 42

64-*The Life of General J.E.B. Stuart*, J. Steven Wilkins, Birmingham, Alabama
65-*Jeb Stuart The Last Cavalier*, Burke Davis, Burford Books, Short Hills, New Jersey, 1957, p. 70
66-*Major General James E. B. Stuart,* Adelle H. Mitchell, p. 169
67-*Major General James E. B. Stuart,* Adelle H. Mitchell, p. 298
68-*Major General James E. B. Stuart,* Adelle H. Mitchell, p. 146
69-*Major General James E. B. Stuart,* Adelle H. Mitchell, p. 318
70-*Stonewall*, John Dwyer, Broadman & Holman, Nashville, Tenn., 1998, p. 553
71-*The Life of General J.E.B. Stuart*, J. Steven Wilkins, Birmingham, Alabama
72-*The Life of General J.E.B. Stuart*, J. Steven Wilkins, Birmingham, Alabama
73-*The Letters of J.E.B. Stuart* – Courtesy of the Stuart Family
74-*The Life of General J.E.B. Stuart*, J. Steven Wilkins, Birmingham, Alabama
75-*Jeb Stuart The Last Cavalier*, Burke Davis, Burford Books, Short Hills, New Jersey, 1957, p. 87-88
76-*The Life of General J.E.B. Stuart*, J. Steven Wilkins, Birmingham, Alabama
77-*The Life of General J.E.B. Stuart*, J. Steven Wilkins, Birmingham, Alabama
78-*Boy in the Saddle*, Gertrude Winders, Howard W. Sams & Co., Inc., New York, 1959, p. 30
79-*The Letters of J.E.B. Stuart* – Courtesy of the Stuart Family
80-*The Letters of J.E.B. Stuart* – Courtesy of the Stuart Family
81-*Boy in the Saddle*, Gertrude Winders, Howard W. Sams & Co., Inc., New York, 1959, p. 31
82-*The Life of General J.E.B. Stuart*, J. Steven Wilkins, Birmingham, Alabama
83-*The Letters of J.E.B. Stuart* – Courtesy of the Stuart Family
84-*Jeb Stuart The Last Cavalier*, Burke Davis, Burford Books, Short Hills, New Jersey, 1957, p. 87

85-*Jeb Stuart The Last Cavalier*, Burke Davis, Burford Books, Short Hills, New Jersey, 1957
86-*Jeb Stuart The Last Cavalier*, Burke Davis, Burford Books, Short Hills, New Jersey, 1957, p. 236
87-*Stonewall*, John Dwyer, Broadman & Holman, Nashville, Tenn., 1998, p. 405
88-Major H. B. McClellan, October 27, 1880, Virginia House of Delegates
89-*Jeb Stuart The Last Cavalier*, Burke Davis, Burford Books, Short Hills, New Jersey, 1957, p. 158
90-*The Life of General J.E.B. Stuart*, J. Steven Wilkins, Birmingham, Alabama
91-*The Life of General J.E.B. Stuart*, J. Steven Wilkins, Birmingham, Alabama
92- *Jeb Stuart The Last Cavalier*, Burke Davis, Burford Books, Short Hills, New Jersey, 1957, p. 410
93-*Jeb Stuart The Last Cavalier*, Burke Davis, Burford Books, Short Hills, New Jersey, 1957, p. 410
94-*Jeb Stuart The Last Cavalier*, Burke Davis, Burford Books, Short Hills, New Jersey, 1957, p. 410
95-*The Life of General J.E.B. Stuart*, J. Steven Wilkins, Birmingham, Alabama
96-*The Letters of J.E.B. Stuart* – Courtesy of the Stuart Family
97-*The Life of General J.E.B. Stuart*, J. Steven Wilkins, Birmingham, Alabama
98-*The Life of J.E.B. Stuart*, Mary L. Williamson, Christian Liberty Press, pg. 22
99-*The Life of General J.E.B. Stuart*, J. Steven Wilkins, Birmingham, Alabama
100-*The Life of J.E.B. Stuart*, Mary L. Williamson, Christian Liberty Press, p. 3
101-http://www.civilwarhome.com/cmhstuartbio.htm
102-*The Life of J.E.B. Stuart*, Mary L. Williamson, Christian Liberty Press, p. 3
103-*Major General James E. B. Stuart,* Adelle H. Mitchell, p. 397
104-Letter from Col. J.E.B. Stuart IV
105-*The Letters of J.E.B. Stuart* – Courtesy of the Stuart Family
106-*The Life of General J.E.B. Stuart*, J. Steven Wilkins, Birmingham, Alabama

107-*Major General James E. B. Stuart,* Adelle H. Mitchell, p. 253
108-*Major General James E. B. Stuart,* Adelle H. Mitchell, p. 327
109-*Major General James E. B. Stuart,* Adelle H. Mitchell, p. 327
110-*Major General James E. B. Stuart,* Adelle H. Mitchell, p. 304
111-*The Letters of J.E.B. Stuart* – Courtesy of the Stuart Family
112-*Jeb Stuart The Last Cavalier*, Burke Davis, Burford Books, Short Hills, New Jersey, 1957, p. 237
113-*Jeb Stuart The Last Cavalier*, Burke Davis, Burford Books, Short Hills, New Jersey, 1957, p.313
114-*General J.E.B. Stuart*, League of the South Lecture Series Tapes
115-*J.E.B. Stuart's Personal Poetry Book* – Compliments of the Stuart Family
116-*Corruption Optimi Pessima*, Rev. Dick Jones, Christ Presbyterian Church, New Braunfels, Texas, 2004
117-*The Life of J.E.B. Stuart*, Mary L. Williamson, Christian Liberty Press, p. 118
118- *Jeb Stuart The Last Cavalier*, Burke Davis, Burford Books, Short Hills, New Jersey, 1957, p. 415
119-http://www.swcivilwar.com/Stuart_FrayserTribute.html
120-*Jeb Stuart The Last Cavalier*, Burke Davis, Burford Books, Short Hills, New Jersey, 1957, p. 415
121-*Jeb Stuart The Last Cavalier*, Burke Davis, Burford Books, Short Hills, New Jersey, 1957, p. 415
122-*Jeb Stuart The Last Cavalier*, Burke Davis, Burford Books, Short Hills, New Jersey, 1957, p. 415
123-*Jeb Stuart The Last Cavalier*, Burke Davis, Burford Books, Short Hills, New Jersey, 1957, p. 415
124-*The Life of J.E.B. Stuart*, Mary L. Williamson, Christian Liberty Press, p. 120
125-*Southern Historical Society Papers - Volume VII – No 2*, February 1878
126-*Jeb Stuart The Last Cavalier*, Burke Davis, Burford Books, Short Hills, New Jersey, 1957, p. 417
127-*Jeb Stuart The Last Cavalier*, Burke Davis, Burford Books, Short Hills, New Jersey, 1957, p. 417
128- Psalm 23

129-*Jeb Stuart The Last Cavalier*, Burke Davis, Burford Books, Short Hills, New Jersey, 1957, p. 418
130-*Jeb Stuart The Last Cavalier*, Burke Davis, Burford Books, Short Hills, New Jersey, 1957, p. 417
131-2 Corinthians 5:8
132-http://www.spartacus.schoolnet.co.uk/USACWstuart.htm
133-Telephone interview with Col. J.E.B. Stuart IV
134-http://www.civilwarhome.com/cmhstuartbio.htm
135-http://www.nrbookservice.com/bookpage.asp?prod_cd=C5427
136-*The Life of J.E.B. Stuart*, Mary L. Williamson, Christian Liberty Press, p. 53
137-*The Autobiography of O. O. Howard*, The Baker and Taylor Company, 1907
138-*The Life of J.E.B. Stuart*, Mary L. Williamson, Christian Liberty Press, p. 121
139-*General J.E.B. Stuart*, League of the South Lecture Series Tapes
140-*General J.E.B. Stuart*, League of the South Lecture Series Tapes
141-Major H. B. McClellan, October 27, 1880, Virginia House of Delegates
142-*The Life of General J.E.B. Stuart*, J. Steven Wilkins, Birmingham, Alabama
143-*The Life of General J.E.B. Stuart*, J. Steven Wilkins, Birmingham, Alabama
144-*The Life of General J.E.B. Stuart*, J. Steven Wilkins, Birmingham, Alabama
145-*The Life of J.E.B. Stuart*, Mary L. Williamson, Christian Liberty Press, p. 67
146-*Summer 2004 Supplement,* Sons of Confederate Veterans, p. 8
147-Telephone interview with Col. J.E.B. Stuart IV
148-Ephesians 2:8-9
149-*The Letters of J.E.B. Stuart* – Courtesy of the Stuart Family
150-Telephone interview with Col. J.E.B. Stuart IV

The Stuart Family Coat of Arms

Salvation Through Christ's Redemption

Printed in Great Britain
by Amazon